REALLY

SCOTTISH
JOKES

Mckinseys
— Tartan
— Large checks

Jack Shaw
Christie sentences
Finishing

Other titles in this series:

REALLY WICKED

SCOTTISH JOKES

Compiled by David Brown

MICHAEL O'MARA BOOKS LTD

First published in Great Britain in 1998
by Michael O'Mara Books Limited
9 Lion Yard
Tremadoc Road
London SW4 7NQ

A CIP catalogue record for this book is available from the British Library

ISBN 1-85479-378-0

1 3 5 7 9 10 8 6 4 2

Cover design by Powerfresh

Designed and typeset by Design 23

Printed and bound in Great Britain by Cox & Wyman, Reading, Berks.

A WEE DRAM

Ben MacTaggert, a farmer in the Scottish highlands, was apprehended by the local constabulary after a routine inspection of his croft revealed an illicit whisky still.

MacTaggert appeared in court next day to face charges of evading excise duty and the illegal manufacture of alcoholic spirits. Summing up the facts of the case before pronouncing judgement the magistrate declared:

"Mr MacTaggert, you have been found in possession of apparatus commonly used in the distillation of alcoholic substances. Although this equipment was unused, and no trace of spirits could be found on your premises, the intent of the apparatus should be clear to all, and I am obliged to find you guilty of all the charges brought before you in this court. Before I pronounce sentence, do you have anything to say in mitigation of your offence?"

MacTaggert glowered at the magistrate and replied "Your Honour, if ye can convict me of moonshining just because I hae the equipment, ye'd better convict me of adultery as well, because I hae the equipment for that tae!"

A Scotsman decided to have a wee celebration at his pub, and ended up drinking until 2 am! He staggered home, and after several tries with his key, got in though the front door. Afraid of waking up his wife, he took off his shoes and started tip-toeing up the stairs, one by one.

Half way up, he fell over backwards and landed flat on his bottom. This wouldn't have been so bad, except that he'd shoved a couple of bottles of beer in his back pockets. The pieces of broken glass splintered right into the skin of his behind, but because he was so drunk, he didn't feel a thing.

A few minutes later, as he was getting undressed, he noticed blood on his shirt-tails, and checked his rear in the bathroom mirror. The sight that met his eyes was horrific, but he did his best to patch it up, and fell into bed.

The next morning he woke up with a massive hangover and an aching bottom. As he tried to recall what had happened to him his wife came into the bedroom.

"Well, ye must have been in a right state last night. So where did ye get tae?"

"What do ye mean, woman? I only had a few wee drams!"

"A few wee drams? that's a laugh! More like a few bottles! Paralytic! That's what ye were!"

"What makes ye so sure, woman?" he replied.

"Well" she said "my first big clue was when I found all those sticking plasters on the bathroom mirror this morning!"

Q. What's the difference between a Scottish wedding and a Scottish funeral?
A. At the funeral there's one less drunk.

Scottish seven course meal....
A pint of whisky and a six pack.

Three Glasgow mice are at a bar, drinking endless shots of whisky and boasting about how tough they are. The first mouse knocks back a shot and says,

"Let me tell you how tough I am: I spot a trap, go for the cheese and when it snaps I grab the bar and bench-press it twenty times or so before I get out of there!"

The second mouse knocks back a shot, demands a re-fill and says, "Think that's tough, eh, Jimmy? Let me tell you, when I find a pile of mouse poison I just crush it up and snort it like it's cocaine!" So saying, he tosses down his whisky and bangs his shot glass on the bar.

The first two mice stare at their companion, waiting to hear what he's got to say. But he just downs his drink, bangs the glass back on the bar and makes for the door.

"Hey, where d'you think you're going?" they ask him.

"I haven't got time for all this," the third mouse says.

"I'm going home to screw the cat."

It was a hot summer afternoon in a small Scottish village, and all the men were pursuing their favourite hobby – drinking whisky in the pub. Suddenly, the door bursts open and a man comes in panting, his tongue lolling and totally black.

"What happened Mac?" enquired one of the regulars.

"Well," said Mac, "a bottle of whisky fell on the hot tar road."

Q. How many Scotsmen does it take to change a light bulb?
A. 21! One to hold the bulb and 20 to drink until the room spins.

FEELING RATHER SHEEPISH

Q. What do you call a Scotsman with a sheep under his arm?
A. A newlywed.

Q. And what do you call a Scotsman with two sheep under his arms?
A. A pimp.

Q. Why do Scotsmen wear kilts?
A. Because sheep have worked out what the sound of zips mean.

Q. Why do Scotsmen wear kilts?
A. Because wool gets caught in zips.

Q Why do Scotsmen have sex with sheep on the edge of cliffs?
A. Because the sheep push back harder.

Q. What do you call a Scotsman with 100 lovers?
A. A shepherd.

Q. What new uses have the Scots just discovered for sheep?
A. Meat and wool.

Q. What do The Rolling Stones and a Scottish highlander have in common?
A. One sings, "Hey!...You!...Get off of my cloud!"
The other says "Eh!...MacCloud!...Get offa mae ewe."

Q. Why are Scottish racehorses so fast?
A. Because they see what gets done to the sheep.

Q. Why do Scottish farmers wear boots?
A. To put the hind legs of sheep in, of course.

A Scotsman is taking his driving test.
"Can you make a U turn?" says the examiner.
"No," replies the Scotsman, "but I can make its eyes water."

A tourist is on a walking holiday in the Scottish highlands. It's a misty day and, his mind having been on other things, he realizes he is hopelessly lost. It's late in the afternoon and he's desperate to find a village with a pub, where he can have a drink and stay the night.

Luckily, after about half an hour, he spies a passer-by, who turns out to be a local who agrees to show him the way. They set off at a brisk pace.

They pass a beautiful, though clearly quite recently planted, forest. "D'yer see those trees?" asks the guide, "I planted all of them. And d'yer think I'm called Jock the Forester? Am I hell."

A little later, they pass a really pretty, finely built cottage.

"D'yer see that cottage over there?" asks the man again. "I designed and built it all on my own. And d'yer think I'm called Jock the Builder? Am I hell."

Further along, with the village just in view, they pass a fine looking garden surrounded by some magnificent railings.

"D'yer see those railings?" asks the man. "I forged them all by myself. And d'yer think I'm called Jock the Blacksmith? Am I hell." "But," he continued, "you hae sex with just one sheep only once......."

When I visited Scotland, I was walking across the glen when I saw a man holding a sheep with its back legs planted in his wellington boots.

"Are you shearing that sheep?" I asked.

"Nay, laddie," he replied. "Get yer own."

Strange coincidences: is it a coincidence that it was the Scots who cloned a sheep?

Scotland – where men are men and the sheep are nervous.

Almost immediately after he'd arrived in a remote Scottish village, the American journalist noticed a curious shortage of women. Walking into the village pub, he asked one of the locals,

"What do you guys do around here for romance?"

"Ye mean women?" asked the highlander. "We've none here. Around here, folks f**k sheep."

"That's disgusting," cried the journalist. "I've never heard of such moral degradation."

However, after a few months, the journalist was feeling sex-starved and the sheep were looking more and more attractive. So he finally went out and found himself a comely sheep, brought her back to his room, shampooed her and then tied ribbons in her hair.

After a bottle of champagne, he lured the sheep into his bedchamber and released his pent-up frustrations.

Afterwards, he escorted his four-legged lover to the pub for a drink.

As the journalist and his woolly friend entered the pub, a hush fell over the patrons and the anxious couple became the object of many disapproving stares.

"You goddamn bunch of hypocrites!" the journalist yelled. "You've been fornicating with sheep for years, but when I do it, you look at me like I'm some sort of crazy pervert."

One highlander at the back of the crowd spoke up, "Ay, laddie, but that's the chieftain's girlfriend ye've got theer."

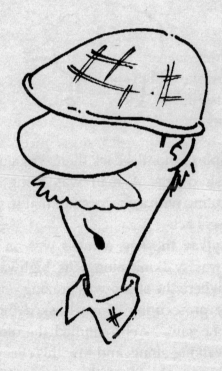

When a tourist coach passes through a small country town in Scotland, one of the passengers noticed a sheep tied to a lamp-post on the corner in the main street.

"Oh that," said the guide, "that's the Recreation Centre."

A couple of months back there was a trial in the Scottish courts. A man was being tried for fornicating with a sheep, since that is, of course, an illegal act.

Anyway the key witness was an old man who was walking along the highway by the farm where the sheep was grazing.

The prosecuting counsel asked the witness what he saw. "Well," replied the old man, "I was walking along, and saw this sheep grazing on the grass. And then this man walks up from behind the sheep, very quietly."

"And then what?" asked the prosecutor.

"Then he raised his kilt and pulled the sheep close." replied the old man.

"And what happened after that?" questioned the prosecutor.

"Well," said the witness, "they sort of shook for a couple of minutes. Then, afterwards, the sheep turned around....an' licked him."

Just then one of the members of the jury leaned over to the juror next to him and whispered, "You know.... a good sheep'll do that."

A Scotsman buys several sheep, hoping to breed them for wool. After several weeks, he notices that none of the sheep are getting pregnant, and he calls a vet for help. The vet tells him that he should try artificial insemination.

The Scotsman doesn't have the slightest idea what this means but, not wanting to display his ignorance, he only asks the vet how he will know when the sheep are pregnant. The vet tells him that they will stop standing around and will, instead, lie down and wallow in the grass when they are pregnant..

The Scotsman hangs up the phone and gives the matter some thought. He comes to the conclusion that artificial insemination means he has to impregnate the sheep.

So, he loads the sheep into his lorry, drives them out into the woods, has sex with them all, brings them back and goes to bed.

Next morning, he wakes and looks out at the sheep. Seeing that they are all still standing around, he concludes that the first try didn't take, and he load them into the lorry again. He drives them out to the woods, has sex with each sheep twice for good measure, brings them back and goes to bed.

Next morning, he wakes to find the sheep still just standing around. One more try, he tells himself, and he proceeds to load them up and drive them out to the woods again. He spends all day having sex with the sheep and, upon returning home, falls into bed exhausted.

The next morning, he's unable even raise himself from the bed to look at the sheep. He asks his wife to look out and tell him if the sheep are laying in the grass.

"Nae," she says, "they're all in the lorry and one of them's honking the horn."

FOUR

LEGGED

FRIENDS

A man went to the pub with his great dane, and when he arrived he left the dog outside, securely tied to a post. A few minutes later, a Scotsman arrived.

Scotsman: "Is that your dog outside?"

First Man: "Yes. What of it?"

Scotsman: "Well, I think my dog's gone an killed him?"

First Man: "Whatever kind of dog have you got that could kill a great dane?"

Scotsman: "I hae a Chihuahua"

First Man: "But how could a Chihuahua kill a great dane?"

Scotsman: "The wee tyke must hae got stuck in his throat!"

The Society of the Paranormal was having a convention in town and there were several hundred delegates attending. The president of the society was at the podium delivering the opening address to all who were there in body and in spirit, and he asked the question:

"Which of you has had the occasion to see a ghost?"

About 40 people raised their hands and the speaker asked them, "Which of you has had the occasion to speak with a ghost?"

This time about 30 delegates raised their hands.

The speaker then posed a third question,

"Which of you has had the occasion to have actually touched a ghost?" in answer to which about ten hands were waved about. The speaker paused for a moment, and then delivered yet another query,

"Which of you has had the occasion to have sex with a ghost?" In the far corner of the auditorium a lone hand was raised. The speaker then said, "Would the usher please escort that individual, with his hand raised, to the podium? I simply must enquire further."

After a few moments delay the individual,

who incidentally turned out to be a wee Scotsman in full kilt and highland regalia, was brought forward to the stage.

When the Scot arrived at the podium, the speaker asked him, "Well, Sir, tell us what it was like to have sex with a ghost," to which the man replied, "Ghost? Laddie, I thought ye said goat."

FOREIGN

AFFAIRS

The American millionaire grew increasingly concerned when alcohol started vanishing from his mansion shortly after he'd hired a new butler, so he decided to confront him.

Faced with his employer's suspicions, the butler said,

"I'll have you know, I come from a long line of honest Englishmen!"

"To be perfectly frank," replied the millionaire, "it's not your English forebears which concern me but your Scottish extraction."

An Englishman, an Irishman and a Scot go out to a pub and order three pints. They each find a fly floating on the top of their mugs.

The Englishman says, "Bartender, can I have a spoon?" and quietly removes the fly from his pint.

The Irishman says, "Get out of there!" and flicks the fly away with a finger.

The Scot picks up the fly with his fingers and says, "Alright ya wee beastie. Spit it out! Now!"

An Englishman and a Scotsman were standing on a corner talking when an Irishman walked up. "You know what?" said the Irishman, "I just went into that pub over there, ordered a pint, played a round of darts and when I walked out of the pub the barman called to me to pay up. So I told him I paid when I got my pint. Well, he didn't say any more, so I got a free drink!"

The Englishman liked the idea so much he went into the pub himself and did the same thing as the Irishman. Sure enough, he came out and told the Irishman and the Scotsman that the barman had said nothing to him either.

The Scotsman decided to give it a try himself. He went in and ordered a pint. As he was chatting to the barman, the man said that two blokes had just walked out without paying. "So why didn't you say anything to them?" asked the Scotsman. "I'm not looking for trouble" replied the barman.

The Scotsman replied "Well, it's getting late, so if you'll give me my change, I'll be going home now!"

Two English ladies were discussing their holiday plans in a teashop. At the next table sat a nice little Scots lady.

"We're planning a lovely holiday in Devon this year" said the first English lady.

"Oh! You shouldn't do that" said her friend "there are hordes of Scots there. It'll be awful!"

"Dear me!" her friend replied "And where will you be going?"

"Salisbury."

"But Salisbury is simply crawling with Scots," the first lady objected.

At this point the dear little Scots lady could hold her tongue no longer. "Why don't ye both go tae hell" she suggested "There'll be no Scots there!"

A Scotsman and an Englishman lived next door to each other. The Scotsman owned a hen and each morning he would look in his garden and pick up one of his hen's eggs for breakfast.

One day he looked into his garden and saw that the hen had laid an egg in the Englishman's garden. He was about to go next door when he saw the Englishman pick up the egg.

The Scotsman ran up to the Englishman and told him that the egg belonged to him because he owned the hen. The Englishman disagreed because the egg was laid on his property.

They argued for a while until finally the Scotsman said, "In my family we normally solve disputes by the following actions: I kick you in the balls and time how long it takes for you to get back up. Then you kick me in the balls and time how long it takes for me to get up. Whoever gets up quicker wins the egg."

The Englishman agreed to this and so the Scotsman put on the heaviest pair of boots he could find. He took a few steps back, then ran towards the Englishman and kicked him as hard as he could in the balls. The Englishman fell to the floor clutching his groin, howling in agony for 30 minutes.

Eventually the Englishman stood up and said, "Now it's my turn to kick you."

The Scotsman said, "Keep the f***king egg."

Q. What's the difference between a Scotsman and an Englishman?

A. If you let a cow loose in their front gardens the Englishman will moan to his wife: "Come here quickly and help me get rid of this horrible cow that is ruining my beautiful lawn."

The Scotsman will call to his wife saying; "Come here quickly! There's a cow on the grass and it needs milking."

An Englishman, an Irishman and a Scotsman went into a pub together. The Englishman stood a round, the Irishman stood a round and the Scotsman stood around.

A condom company wanted to know what was the optimum number of condoms to put into a box, so they decided to conduct a survey.

They asked an Englishman how many he thought there should be and he said, "Seven". They asked him why he had chosen that number and he said there should be one for each day of the week.

Then the condom company asked an Irishman the same question and he answered, "Nine". They asked him why he had chosen that number and he said there should be one for every week day, two for Saturdays and two for Sundays.

Finally the condom company asked a Scotsman how many condoms there should be in a box and to their amazement he replied, "12." When they asked him why he had chosen that number he said, "January, February, March..."

An Englishman was in a restaurant in Glasgow when he suddenly suffered a severe burst of coughing and sneezing. He sneezed so violently that his false teeth flew out of his mouth and dropped on the floor, where they broke at the feet of a Scotsman.

"Don't worry, sir," said the Scotsman. "My brother will soon get you a new pair and it will be much cheaper than from an English dentist. And, what's more, he can provide a suitable set almost immediately."

The Englishman couldn't believe his luck and gladly accepted the Scotsman's offer.

The Scotsman left the restaurant and returned ten minutes later with a set of false teeth which he handed to the Englishman.

"That's fantastic!" exclaimed the Englishman, trying the teeth. "They fit perfectly. Your brother must be a very clever dentist."

"Oh, he's not a dentist, said the Scotsman. "He's an undertaker."

There is a beautiful deserted island in the middle of the Ocean where the following people are stranded:

Two Italian men and one Italian woman
Two French men and one French woman
Two Greek men and one Greek woman
Two English men and one English woman
Two Bulgarian men and one Bulgarian woman
Two Swedish men and one Swedish woman
Two Australian men and one Australian woman
Two Welsh men and one Welsh woman
Two Scottish men and one Scottish woman

One month later on this beautiful deserted island, the situation was as follows:

* The first Italian man killed the other for the Italian woman.
* The two French men and the French woman are living happily together in a 'ménage à trois.'
* The two German men have a strict weekly schedule of when they alternate with the German woman.
* The two Greek men are sleeping with each

other and the Greek woman is cleaning and cooking for them.

* The two English men are waiting for someone to introduce them to the English woman.

* The Bulgarian men took one look at the endless ocean, one look at the Bulgarian woman and started swimming.

* The two Swedish men are contemplating the virtues of suicide, while the Swedish woman keeps on bitching about her body being her own and about the true nature of feminism. But at least it's not snowing and the taxes are low.

* The Australians are all wankers, so who cares?

* The two Welsh men start searching the island for sheep while the Welsh woman gets friendly with a big banana she's found.

* The two Scottish men set up a distillery. They don't remember if sex is in the picture as things get a bit foggy after the first few litres of coconut-whisky, but at least they're happy knowing that the English aren't getting any.

Did you hear what the English, the Irish and the Scots did when they heard that the world was coming to an end?

The English all went out and got drunk.

The Irish all went to Church.

The Scots had a closing down sale.

An Englishman, an Irishman and a Scotsman are standing in a field. Seeing a cow the other side of the field, the Englishman says,

"Look over there at that fine English cow."

"No, no, that's an Irish cow," exclaims the Irishman.

"No, it's not," says the Scotsman. "It's Scottish – it's got bagpipes underneath."

A Hindu, a Jew and a Scotsman are lost in the woods when they happen across a farm. They knock on the door and ask the farmer if they can stay the night. "Well, sure," the farmer says, "but I only have room for two inside, the third will have to stay in the barn."

The three men look at each other for a moment, and the Jew says, "I'll sleep in the barn." Not two minutes have passed and he comes out and says, "Oy!, I can't sleep in the barn, there are pigs there, it's not kosher."

So the Hindu says, "All is well, sahib, I will sleep in the barn." Two minutes later he comes out and says, "By the many arms of Vishnu, there is a cow in there. I cannot sleep with a cow, it would be against my faith."

The Scotsman says, "Well, that's alright, I'll take thae barn," and off he goes.

Two minutes go by when a sheep comes out......

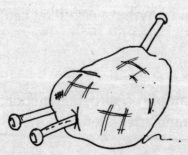

A Scotsman and a Jew went to a restaurant. After a hearty meal, the waitress came up to the table with the bill. To everyone's amazement, the Scotsman was heard to say, "I'll pay it," and he actually did.

The next morning's newspaper carried the news item: "JEWISH VENTRILOQUIST FOUND MURDERED IN BLIND ALLEY."

There are four kinds of people that live in Great Britain:

First there are the Welsh, who pray on their knees and on their neighbours.

Next are the Irish, who don't know what they want, but they'll fight anyone for it.

Then there are the English, who consider themselves self-made men, which relieves the Almighty of any responsibility.

And last are the Scots, who hold onto their children and anything else they can get their hands on.

Give an example of perpetual motion.
A Scot running after a Jew.

During a recent international sports meeting, one of the Scottish track and field coaches was entertaining some friends and colleagues in his hotel room. As so often happens, the libations were used up before it was time to end the festivities.

After receiving directions to the nearest off licence, the Scottish coach left the party. On arriving at the off licence, he noticed that there were only three or four people waiting in the queue.

Immediately ahead of him were two men dressed in military fatigues and heavily bearded. He overheard one of them ordering several bottles of Scotch and rum. Upon being told the value of his purchases, this bearded individual told the shop assistant that he was with Fidel. Immediately the shop assistant produced a book and the individual signed for his purchases. To say that the Scotsman was intrigued would be an understatement.

The other individual in front of the Scotsman proceeded to order at least twice as much as his companion had ordered. Upon receipt of his total, he also told the assistant that he was with Fidel. The same book was brought out and the same procedure followed as had occurred with his companion.

By this time the Scotsman had decided that he was on to a good thing. He ordered numerous bottles of whisky, rum and vodka, together with cartons of cigarettes and boxes of cigars. Upon being presented with his bill, he told the assistant that he was with Fidel.

The assistant told him that he could not be with Fidel.

"Why not?" asked the indignant Scotsman.

"Because you do not have the beard and the big cigar," the assistant replied.

Pausing for only a moment, the Scotsman reached down, lifted up his kilt and proudly announced, "SECRET SERVICE!"

NATURAL GENIUS

The great Texan fire fighter, Red Adair walked into an Aberdeen pub. He'd just spent two weeks putting out a huge fire on a North Sea oil rig and was feeling absolutely shattered.

He ordered a pint of bitter and sat down at a table.

The Scotsman sitting next to him realised that he was an American and said:

"I've been to the States myself, ye ken! I went there last year!"

"Yeah, really!" said Red in a tired voice.

"Och aye! I spent a whole month in California. I went to this concert with the famous country singer Benny Rogers and..."

"Surely you mean KENNY Rogers!" replied Red, looking up at the ceiling.

"Aye! That's right. He sang a duet with a bonnie lass called Polly Darton."

"It's Dolly Parton, not Polly Darton" replied Red, feeling quite exasperated.

The Scotsman realized he was irritating the American, and tried to change the subject.

"Hey! Hae'n't I seen ye on the TV? Ye're famous, aren't ye?"

This made Red feel quite cheered up.

"You sure have! I'm Red Adair!" he announced proudly.

"Red Adair! the REAL Red Adair! So! Are ye still married to Ginger Rogers?"

Q. What's the difference between the New York mafia and the Glasgow mafia?
A. One makes you an offer you can't refuse and the other makes you an offer you can't understand.

Q. What do you get if you cross a Scottish mass murderer with a fish?
A. Jock the Kipper.

A Scotsman was walking along a beach when he happened to notice a bottle lying on the sand. It had obviously been washed ashore.

Thinking it might contain something of value, he picked it up and pulled out the cork.

As soon as he had unstoppered the bottle, a genie popped out in a cloud of smoke and other pyrotechnics.

"Oh, thank you for liberating me, brave sir," quoth the genie. "I have been helplessly trapped in this bottle for 40 millenia. In recompense for your kind deed, I shall grant you three wishes."

"Weel noo, laddie" replied the Scot, thinking carefully "I'd like a wee dram o' the finest whisky."

Immediately, there appeared before him a six gallon container of the very finest whisky.

The Scot immediately opened it and gulped it down, then emitted a hearty belch. Imagine his surprise when, as soon as he had put it down, it magically refilled itself to the top.

"Special feature," explained the genie, "it can never be emptied. Now what would you like for your other two wishes?"

"Why, thank ye very much," exclaimed the Scot. "I'll take two more o' the same."

A Scotsman was caught for speeding and hauled up before the judge.

"What will you take?" asked the judge. "30 days or £30?"

"I think I'll take the money," replied the Scotsman.

Sandy was only five feet tall. He attributed his lack of height to the fact that as a child in Aberdeen he was fed exclusively on condensed milk and shortbread.

THE
CANNY
SCOT

Q. What's the difference between a Scotsman and a coconut?
A. You can always get a drink out of a coconut.

Q. Why do the Scots have double glazed windows?
A. So that their kids can't hear the ice cream vans.

Q. How are the Scots and crime alike?
A. Neither of them pay.

Q. Why do Scottish people refuse to buy refrigerators?
A. They don't believe that the light will go out when you close the door.

Q. Why don't Scotsmen ever have coffee the way they like it?

A. Well, they like it with two lumps of sugar, but if they drink it at home, they only take one lump, and if they drink it while visiting, they always take three lumps.

Scotsman to taxi driver: "How much is it to the airport?"

Taxi driver: "That'll be £5.20."

Scotsman: "And what would it be just for the luggage?"

Taxi driver: "Luggage? that's free, of course!"

Scotsman: "Ok. You take the luggage. I'll just walk!"

Jock was in terrible trouble. His business had gone under, and he was in a serious financial mess. He was so desperate, he decided to turn to God for help, and went to the kirk to pray.

"Oh God! Ye've got tae help me! I've lost mae business and if I don't get some money I'll be losing mae hoose as well. Please let me win the lottery."

Lottery night came, and someone else won.

Jock went back to the kirk.

"Oh God! Please let me win the lottery! I've lost my business, mae hoose and noo I've lost mae car!"

Lottery night came and still Jock had no luck.

Back to the kirk.

"God! Why hae ye forsaken me? I've lost mae business, mae hoose, mae car – and mae wife and bairns are starving! I've never asked ye for anything else before, so why don't ye help me? Why don't ye let me win the lottery?"

At that moment there was a blinding flash of light as the heavens opened. And Jock was confronted with the voice of God himself.

"Jock! Why don't you meet me halfway on this one! Buy a f**king ticket!"

Robbie Macphee went into a barber's shop and asked the barber the price of a haircut.

"Two pounds," said the barber.

"How much is a shave?" asked Macphee.

"One pound," said the barber.

"Shave my head," said Macphee.

You have to be very careful about stereotyping the Scots as mean. There was a letter in the paper the other day from an angry Glasgwegian. It said, "If you print any more jokes about Scotsmen, I shall have to stop borrowing your paper."

Did you hear the one about the Scotsman who died of a broken heart? He was fed up with reading jokes about how mean the Scots are, so he went into his nearest pub and ordered a round for everyone in it.

"That's very kind of you, sir," said the publican. "There must be 50 people in here. I didn't know you Scots were so generous."

The Scotsman was visiting London for the day and found himself in Soho where he called upon a prostitute. After he had spent a couple of hours in bed with her, he gave her two thousand pounds.

"That's incredibly generous of you!" the girl gasped. "No punter has ever paid me so much money before. And yet, from your accent I'd say you were a Scotsman."

"Aye, you're right." the Scotsman replied.

So which part of Scotland are you from?"

"From Edinburgh." the Scotsman replied.

"That's a coincidence," the girl said, "My Dad works in Edinburgh."

"I know," said the Scotsman. "And when he heard I was coming down to London he asked me to bring you a share of his Lottery winnings - two thousand pounds."

Johnson married the most shapely girl in the office, and all his mates envied him, in particular an unmarried young Scot who said one day, "Ye ken, I'd give a hundred pounds to smack the pretty bottom of yon wee wife o'yours."

Johnson was furious and went home raging to his wife about it. But the wife had Scottish blood too, and she said, "Well you know, the furniture isn't paid for yet, and I could do with a fur coat. What's a few smacks on the bottom, when all's said and done?"

Eventually she wore her husband down and finally he was obliged to tell Jock that he could smack his wife;'s bare bottom for a hundred pounds, but only on the condition that he had to be there while it happened. Then he could make sure there was no funny business.

So the three of them got together on a Saturday night in the Johnson's bedroom and the blushing wife pulled down her knickers, stepped out of them and bent over the bed.

Jock lifted her skirt up and started to gently stroke her bottom saying, "What beautiful curves! What a delicate shade of pink! What charming dimples! how lovely and firm it is!" And all the while he was stroking and caressing while Johnson was becoming more and more enraged.

When Jock suddenly produced a camera from his pocket and started taking photographs, Johnson finally shouted, "Get on with it, will you? Smack her right now or the whole thing's off!"

"Och no!" said Jock, "I could never bring myself to smack such a beautiful bottom as this one. And besides, it would cost me a hundred pounds if I did!"

Have you heard the one about the Grand Canyon having been started by a Scotsman who lost a penny in a ditch?

A Scotsman is a man who goes to a wedding with a broom and brings home the rice for dinner.

Tea Time in Scotland:

"Dad!" called the little boy, "There's boiling water coming out of the radiator!"

"Don't waste it!" shouted his Dad in reply. "Throw in a tea bag."

Scotsman: A man who stays at home and lets his mind wander.

My uncle is a Scotsman. He runs his toothpaste tube through the wringer but my auntie has hers run over by a bus.

Jock was out of cigarettes so he decided to ask his friend Sandy for a match. When he had got the match he searched his pockets and said, "I seem to have forgotten my cigarettes."

"In that case you won't be needing the match," replied Sandy.

The Scotsman comes to his friend in tears. "My beautiful comb," he cries. "I broke a tooth on it and now I can't use it any more. What am I going to do? Now I'll have to buy another one."

"Well," said his friend, "you don't need to buy another just because you lost one tooth on your comb."

"But you don't understand," said the Scotsman, "it was the last tooth."

Mike is living in Glasgow and drops in on his friend, Jimmy, who lives down the road.

When he arrives Jimmy is stripping all the wallpaper off the walls in his living room.

"Oh, you're decorating," says Mike.

"Nay, laddie," says Jimmy, "I'm moving."

THE
GAY
SCOT

Q. How do you separate the men from the boys in Scotland?

A. With a crowbar.

Q. What do you call two famous gay Scotsmen?
A. Ben Dover and Phil MacRevis.

Richard had been working at the stock exchange for 12 years and the stress finally got to him. He decided to leave his job and buy a cottage in the middle of nowhere, right up in the highlands of Scotland.

For months he didn't see a single person, but then, one evening, as he was contemplating the glorious view out of his window, there came a knock on the front door. Standing on the doorstep was an enormous, ginger-haired Scotsman.

"The name's Malcolm. I live over the other side of the glen and I'm throwing a party on Saturday night. I thought you might like to come."

"Thanks very much," said Richard. "After being alone for six months I'm ready to meet some locals. It's a very welcome invitation."

"Good." said Malcolm, smiling through his huge beard. "I should warn you though, there'll be some serious drinking done."

"No problem," says Richard. "After working in the City for 15 years I can drink as well as the next man."

"Most likely there'll be a punch-up during the course of the evening, too," says Malcolm.

"Don't worry about me," said Richard. "I'm pretty easy-going and anyway, I can look after myself."

Malcolm started to leave, but then turned and said, "One other thing – I've seen some pretty wild sex at these parties before now."

"Great!" says Richard. "What time should I come over?"

"Whatever time suits you," says Malcolm. "After all, it's only going to be the two of us."

THE
BONNY
PIPES

"I just found out why the bagpipes make the Scotsmen brave in war."

"Why is that?"

"They'd rather die than have to hear them."

A Scotsman was seriously ill in hospital. His doctors were very afraid that this was to be the end of him, since there was nothing that they could do to make him healthy.

His doctor came to his bedside and asked him if there was anything he could do to make him comfortable during his final hours.

"If I could hear the pipes one more time, it would make me very happy, doctor."

So the doctor arranged for a piper to come into the ward and play for the dying man.

As soon as the Scot heard the pipes the colour came back into his cheeks, his eyes became bright, his breathing became easier and he got up and danced around the ward. He was completely cured.

Later, while recounting the story over lunch

the doctor confessed that this was a miracle cure that he really couldn't explain.

"I was amazed!" he said "When the pipes began to play, the man was completely cured. The only problem though was that two Englishmen who'd just come in for checkups died on the spot!"

There are many theories about the bagpipes, otherwise known as the missing link between music and noise.

The truth is that they were given to the Scots by the Irish as a joke....but the Scots haven't seen the joke yet!

THE

BRAW

KILT

A Scotsman, wearing a kilt, was walking down a country path after finishing off a considerable amount of whisky at a local pub. As he staggered down the road, he felt quite sleepy and decided to take a nap with his back against a tree.

As he slept, two young lasses walked down the road and heard the Scotsman snoring loudly. They saw him, and one said, "I've always wondered what a Scotsman wears under his kilt." She boldly walked over to the sleeping man, raised his kilt, and saw what nature had provided him at his birth.

Her friend said, "Well, he has solved a great mystery for us. He must be rewarded!" So, she took a blue ribbon from her hair, and gently tied it around what nature had provided the Scotsman, and the two walked away.

Some time later, the Scotsman was awakened by the call of nature, and walked around to the other side of the tree to relieve himself. He raised his kilt...and saw where the blue ribbon was tied.

After several moments of bewilderment, the Scotsman said,"I dinna know where y'been laddie...but it's nice ta' know y'won first prize!"

Sandy McTavish was wandering around the local department store when he spotted a bolt of the McTavish clan tartan at a spectacularly low price. As his own kilt was six years old and very shabby, he was delighted, and approached the shop assistant.

"Lassie! I'd like a yard and a half of that McTavish tartan. I'll be needing a new kilt.

" Of course, sir. Could you show me which tartan you want?"

Sandy walked over to the display table and showed her the plaid.

"Sorry sir, that tartan only comes in three-yard lengths."

"Ye dinna understand, lassie! I just need a yard and a half!"

"I'm very sorry sir! But the plaid comes in three yard lengths. Why don't you use a yard and a half to make your kilt, and use the other half to make a scarf for your girlfriend?"

It was clear to Sandy that he was going to have to buy the whole three yards if he was going to get a new kilt.

"All right, lassie! I'll take the three yards!"

He took the plaid home and made a new kilt for himself and a scarf for his girl friend. He was so pleased with the kilt, that he decided to go over to her house to show it off. He'd keep the scarf as a surprise for later.

He'd forgotten that in the six years since he'd worn his old kilt he'd lost over two stone in weight. But he'd used the same pattern for the new one. As he was rushing to his girl friend's house, the kilt slipped over his hips and was gone. In his excitement he didn't even notice. He got to her door and knocked.

She saw him from the window and opened the front door. As she did, he threw open his coat and said:

"Well! Hae de ye like that?"

She stared for a moment and replied "I like it just fine, Sandy!"

"Aye, lassie, and there's another yard and a half ye'll be gettin' for Christmas!"

I've just washed my kilt and I can't do a fling with it.

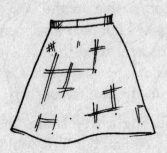

Tourist: "Is anything worn under that kilt?"

Scotsman: "No, everything's in perfect working order."

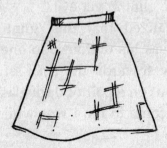

"So you belong to a Scottish regiment. Do you have the right to bear arms?"

"Of course, and we have the right to bare legs."

Mac was courting a wee lassie, and this wee lassie had a wee flat, but Jock could never get any further than the doorstep. Every night he would take her home and ask, "Can I come in for a wee while, Mary?"

And Mary always replied, "Nae, nae, Jock, I can see the glint in yer eye."

Jock realized that this 'glint in the eye' business was his undoing, so one night, as he took Mary towards the door of her flat, he sneakily put on a pair of dark glasses.

"Can I come in for a wee while, Mary?" he asked.

"Nae, nae, Jock." she replied.

"But Mary!" Jock exclaimed, "Ye canna see the glint in me eye!"

"Nae, nae, Jock," said Mary, "but I can see the tilt o' yer kilt!"

How do you tell a Scotsman's clan?

You put your hand up his kilt and if you feel a couple of quarter pounders, you'll know he's a Macdonald.

An American tourist sees a Scotsman in a kilt. She has always been curious to know what is worn under a kilt so, summoning up her courage, she asks him.

The Scotsman replies that, if she really wants to know, she is welcome to feel under his kilt in order to satisfy her curiosity. So she gingerly places her hand under his kilt... "Oh, it's gruesome," she shrieks, quickly removing her hand.

"Aye," replies the Scotsman, "and if you'd like to try it again, you'll find it's gruesome more."

The Director of the Scottish Tartans Museum, Dr Hamish MacDonald was in America. An old lady fixed her gaze on his 17th century sporran and asked, "What, exactly, do you keep in your scrotum?"

THE SPORTING LIFE

Angus and Hamish were sitting in the pub having a few drams when some fishermen walked in with some huge trout.

The Scotsmen were really impressed at the size of the trout. Several drams later, they walked unsteadily up to the fishermen and asked where they got the fish.

"Oh! Nothing to it!" replied the men. All you have to do is go down to the bridge. One of you holds the other by the ankles until he catches the fish.

By this time Angus and Hamish had had a few more drams and decided this would be a great idea. So off they went to the bridge.

Angus held Hamish by the ankles, and after about 20 minutes he asked him if he'd caught anything.

"Nae luck yet!" replied Hamish.

After another 20 minutes, he asked again and got the same reply.

More time passed and suddenly Hamish yelled out "Angus! Pull me up quick! Pull me up! Pull me up! "

"Hae ye got one?" shouted Angus, excited.

"Nae, I hae'n't. There's a train coming!"

Q. Do you know why there are 18 holes on a golf course?

A. Because that's how long it took the Scots, who invented the game, to finish their bottle of whisky!

The Scotsman wore a black band on his sleeve...he was in mourning for a lost golf ball.

The story goes like this: a Scotsman named Angus played the same golf ball for over 25 years. One day, the unthinkable happened and Angus lost his ball. After searching high and low, for hours on end, he gave up and walked into the golf shop, totally disgusted.

"Well, Jamie," he announced, "here I am again!"

Q. What's the difference between a golf pro and a Scotsman?
A. A golf pro gives tips.

A Scotsman gets shipwrecked and washed up on a small island. When he wakes up on the beach, he sees a beautiful girl standing, looking down at him.

"Would you like something to eat?" she asks.

"Och, lassie," the Scotsman says, weakly, "I havna' eaten a bite in a week noo, and I'm verra, verra hungry."

She runs off into the woods along the beach and returns a little while later with a huge helping of haggis which the Scotsman starts to devour.

When he's finished his meal she says, "Would you like something to drink?"

"Och, aye, lassie, the haggis has made me verra, verra thirsty and I wad love something to drink!"

Off she runs into the woods again and this time she re-appears with a bottle of 50-year-old single malt whisky. The Scotsman begins to think he's died and gone to heaven, and then the girl leans down close to him and whispers softly in his ear, "Would you like to play around?"

"Och, lassie!" he exclaims. "Don't you be telling me ye've got a golf course here, too!"

A man up in Scotland called on a garage where they did a big business in tyres and tyre repairs. Somewhat sheepishly he asked if the manager would see him in his private office. He then pulled from his wallet a rather tatty rubber condom and said, "How much will ye charge to vulcanize a patch on yon?"

The manager was rather surprised but said nothing until he had thoroughly examined the object.

"About 50p but, as you can buy a new one for 60p, I don't see much point in it."

"Verra guid," said the client, "Ah wull let ye know in a day or two. Ah'll have to ask them."

"Them? Ask them? Ask who, exactly?" enquired the manager.

"Them at the Aberdeen Golf Club."

Q. Why did the Scottish horse rider buy just one spur?

A. Because he reckoned that wherever one side of the horse went, the other side would follow.

A Scotsman went hunting duck early one morning and, although he had many chances, he kept missing his shots.

Every time he missed, he took a big dram from his flask and gradually got drunker and drunker. Finally he thought he'd have one more try, aimed his gun at a bird, missed and hit a frog instead. As he picked up the lifeless body of the frog he said, "Well, at least I knocked the feathers off it."

Robbie McPherson and Jimmy MacDonald were doing some mountaineering in Switzerland when Robbie slipped and fell into a crevice.

"Run down to the village as fast as you can, and get some rope," he shouted to Jimmy. "I'll try to hang on by my fingernails until you get back."

Half an hour passed. Robbie felt his grip gradually weakening. After another 20 minutes, with Robbie now feeling he was close to the end, he heard Jimmy returning.

"Well, did you get the rope?" he shouted painfully.

"No," said Jimmy, "those cheats in the village wanted three pounds for it."

It was another of those taut Celtic v. Rangers matches at Ibrox Park. A mild-mannered little man was accosted by a huge, aggressive looking fan in full regalia. "Well, Jimmy," he snarled menacingly, "are ye a Celtic or a Rangers man?

"Actually, I'm neither," said the little man nervously. "I just enjoy watching football."

"Och, I see," growled the Scot, "a bloody atheist, eh?"

A recent Scottish immigrant in America attends his first baseball game in his new country. After a base hit, he hears the fans roaring, "Run...Run...!"

The next batsman connects heavily with the ball, and the Scotsman stands up with the crowd and yells in his thick Scottish accent, "R-r-run ya bahstahd, r-r-run will ya!"

A third batsman slams a hit and again the Scotsman, obviously pleased with his knowledge of the game, yells, "R-r-run ya bahstahd, r-r-run will ya!"

The next batsman holds his swing at three

and two, and the umpire calls a walk. The Scotsman stands up, yelling,

"R-r-run ya bahstahd, r-r-run will ya!"

The surrounding fans giggle amongst themselves, and the Scotsman sits, confused. A neighbouring fan notices his confusion and offers an explanation, "He doesn't have to run, he's got four balls."

After this explanation, the Scotsman stands up and yells, "Walk with p-r-r-ride, man!"

WEDDED BLISS

Robbie and his wife Maggie are walking along Princes Street in Edinburgh one evening, window shopping. They stop by a jewellery shop and Maggie says, "I'd really love to have those diamond earrings."

"No problem," says Robbie. And taking a brick out of his pocket, he smashes the window and grabs the earrings. They walk off quickly but soon find themselves outside another jewellery shop, and in the window is a gorgeous, diamond ring.

"Oh, Robbie, just look at that diamond ring! I'd really love to have it," says Maggie.

Robbie looks round to make sure there's no-one around, takes another brick from his pocket, smashes the window and grabs the ring. Again they walk quickly away, and Maggie's thrilled with her earrings and her ring. A little further on they come across yet another jewellery shop and this time there is a fabulous diamond necklace in the window.

"Robbie, Robbie! Just look at that! It goes perfectly with the earrings and the ring. I really want it, in fact I must have it!"

"For God's sake, woman," says Robbie. "D'you think I'm made of bricks?"

"That Scotsman over there has 20 kids."
"Great Scot!"

A handsome young Scotsman got married. That night, after the celebrations were over and the bride and groom had left for their honeymoon night, his father was sitting down at his kitchen table, having a wee dram when the door bursts open and in comes his son.

"What are you doing here, Bobbie? You should be in bed with your bride."

Bobbie said nothing, but poured himself a large glass of whisky and sat there glumly, drinking it.

"Come on, son, tell me what the problem is. Maybe I can help you. If you really love each other there's not much that can't be sorted out."

"Well, Dad," said Bobbie, "she's a virgin."

"You'll have tae send her back then, Bobbie," said his father. "If she's nay good enough for her own family, she certainly isn't good enough for ours."

One day old Maggie asked her husband as they were going to bed, "What will become of us when you canna work any more?"

"Look out the window, woman," said

Charlie, "I own those two cottages and the shop on the corner."

"How d'you manage to buy them, Charlie, when you're on such a low wage?" she asked.

"I've been putting 50p away under the mattress each time you let me make love to you, ever since the day we married."

"Well I never!" Maggie exclaimed.

"Yes, and if you hadna been such a mean, frigid old bitch we'd hae' had two hotels and a pub," he replied.

A Scottish couple made an appointment to go to the doctor. When they were sitting in front of him he asked, "How can I help you?"

"Would you mind watching us have intercourse, Doctor?" the man replied.

The doctor was puzzled but he agreed, and the couple proceeded to have sex in his office. When they had finished they looked at him and he said, "There's absolutely nothing wrong with the way you have intercourse," and he charged them £32 for the consultation.

This happened every week for the next few weeks – the couple would make an appointment at the same time, on the same day, have intercourse, pay the doctor and leave.

Finally, one afternoon, the doctor greeted them as they came into his office and then said, "Excuse me, but I must ask you – what exactly is the problem? What is it that you are trying to find out?"

The man answered, "Nothing. She's married so we can't go to her house. I'm married too, so we can't go to mine either. The Holiday Inn charges £78. We can do it here for £32 and I can get £28 back from BUPA for a visit to the doctor's office."

The old Scotsman, McKelvie, was on his deathbed. His wife, Jean, was sitting beside him, tenderly stroking his brow and she said, "Rory, do you have a last wish at all?"

McKelvie could smell the gingerbread that his wife was baking in the kitchen and whispered, "Could I have just a wee slice of that cake that you're baking, Jean? It smells wonderful."

"I'm sorry, Rory," Jean replied firmly. "That's for after your funeral."

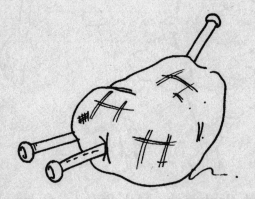